African
Art and Designs
Adult Coloring Book

ZenMaster Coloring Books

Helpful Tips for Coloring

~ Sometimes the colors appear differently on paper than what you would expect. Use the color test page to play with your colors beforehand.

~ If you are using colored pencils make sure to keep them sharp. This helps when coloring smaller areas or details on the page. Fine point sharpies also work great for smaller areas.

~ Speaking of sharpies, make sure you put a scrap piece of paper behind the page you are coloring to keep the markers from bleeding to the next page.

~ When using crayons or pencils start out light. You can always go back and darken later.

~ There are so many tools for coloring: markers, sharpies, crayons, pencils, pastels, and the list goes on. Experiment with what works best for you and your designs. Though it's not necessary, using higher quality coloring utensils makes a difference.

~ If you come to a design that seems overwhelming just pick a place to start and go from there. Once you begin your creativity will quickly take over!! If you get discouraged just take a break and come back to the page later.

~ Remember to practice. Like anything else, the more you do it the better you'll get. It'll become more and more relaxing each time.

~ DON'T FOLLOW THE RULES! It's up to you how you color your designs. Just let your creativity take the lead and HAVE FUN!

COLOR TEST PAGE

COLOR TEST PAGE

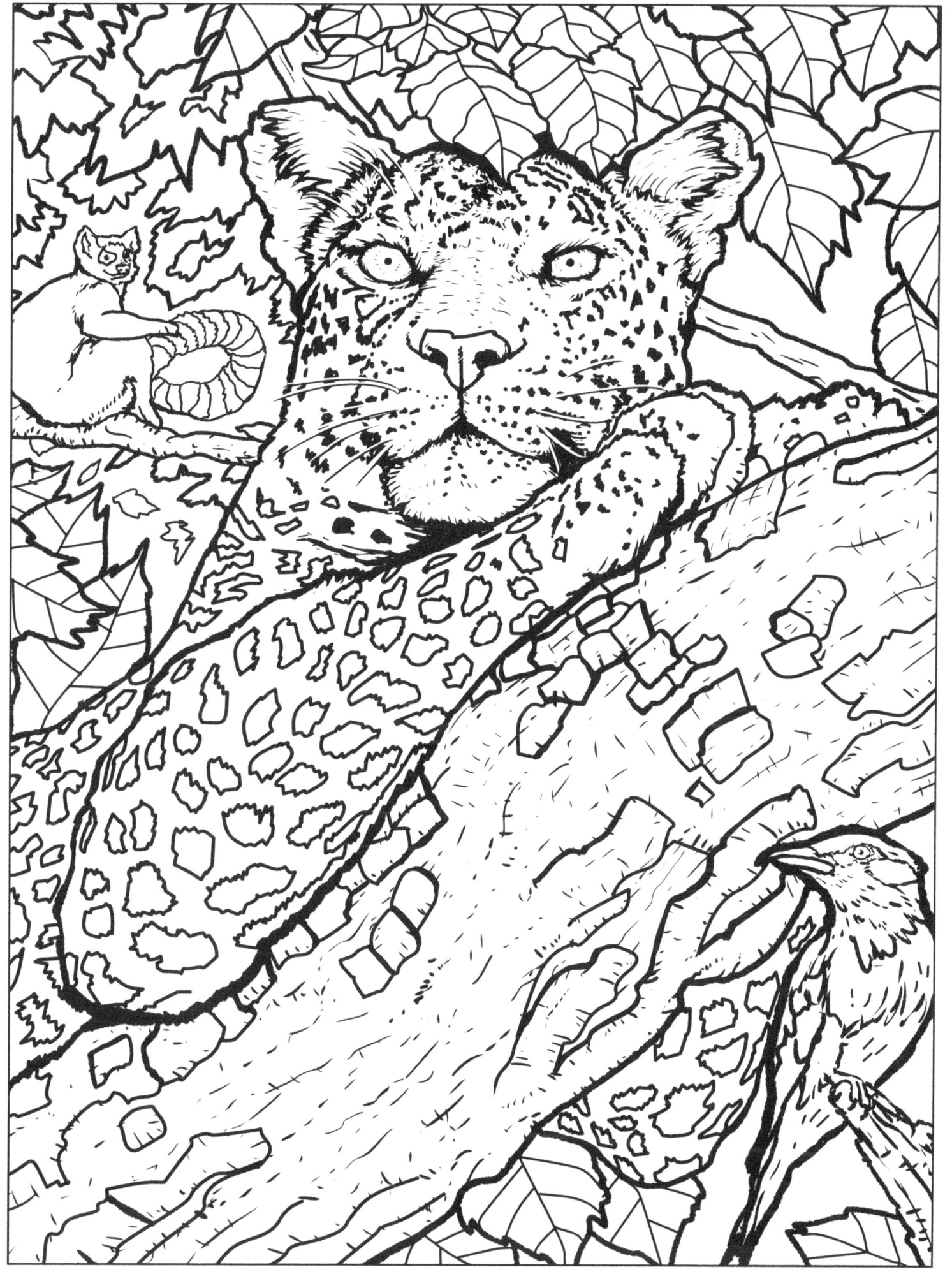

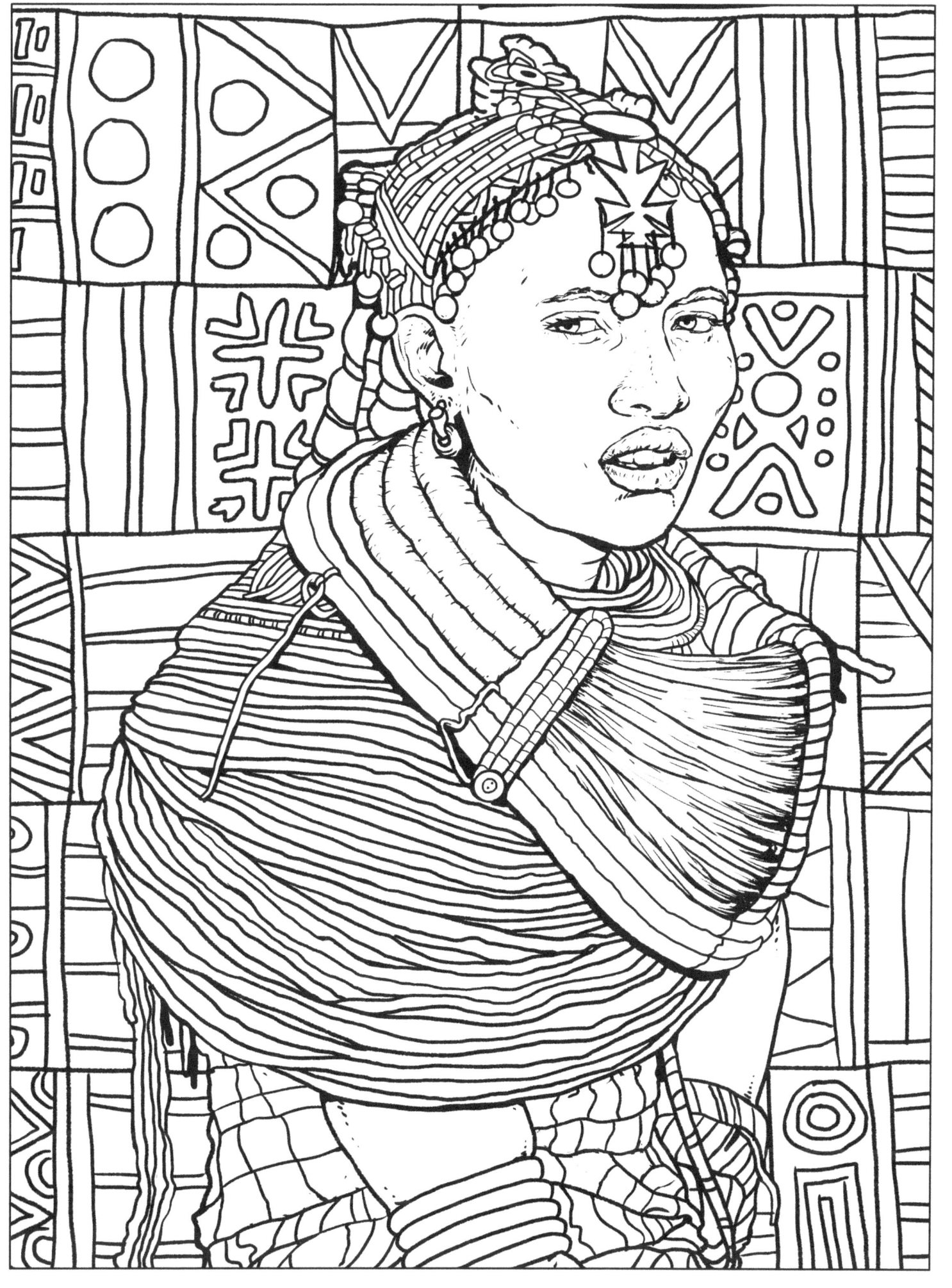

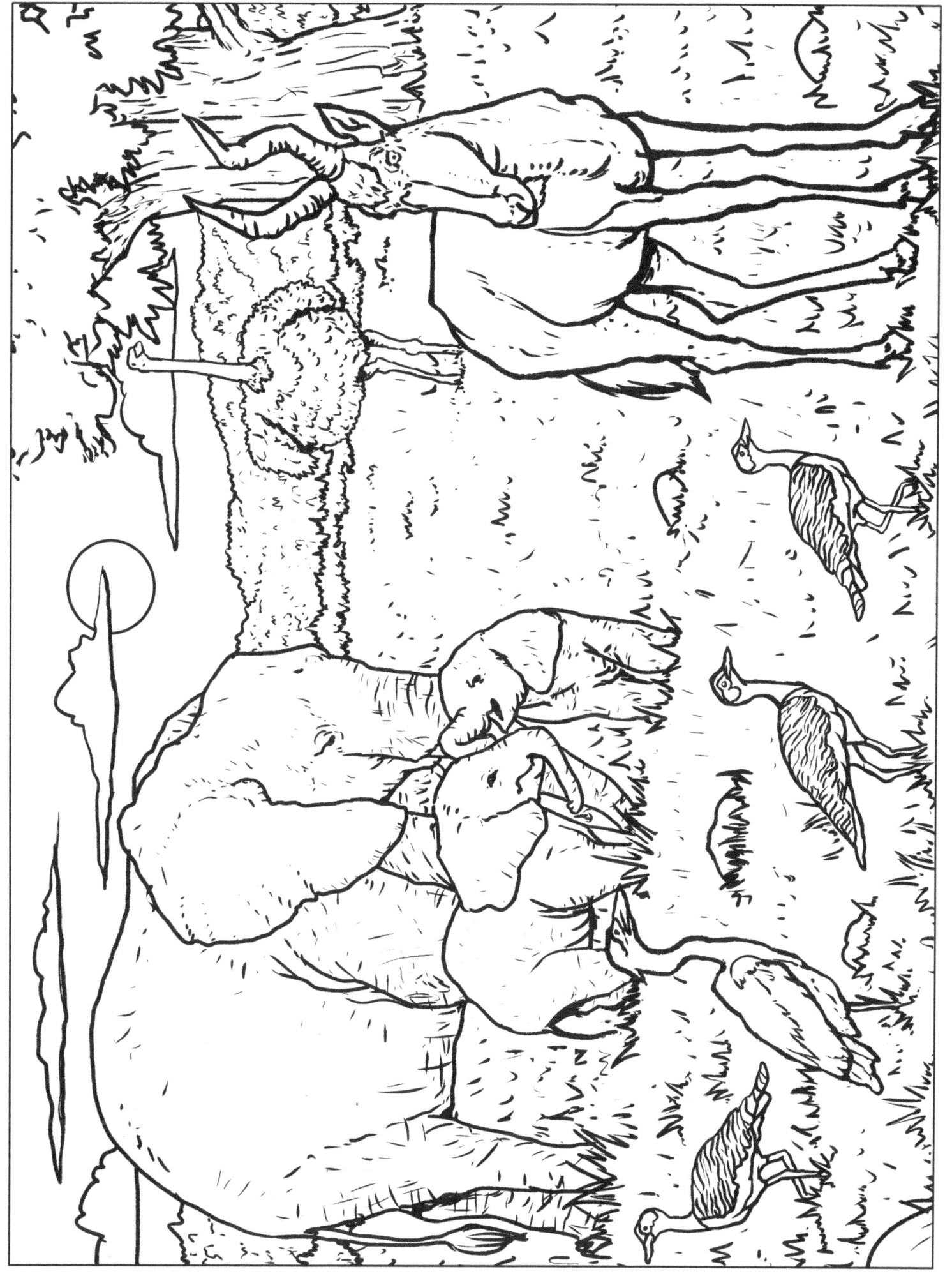

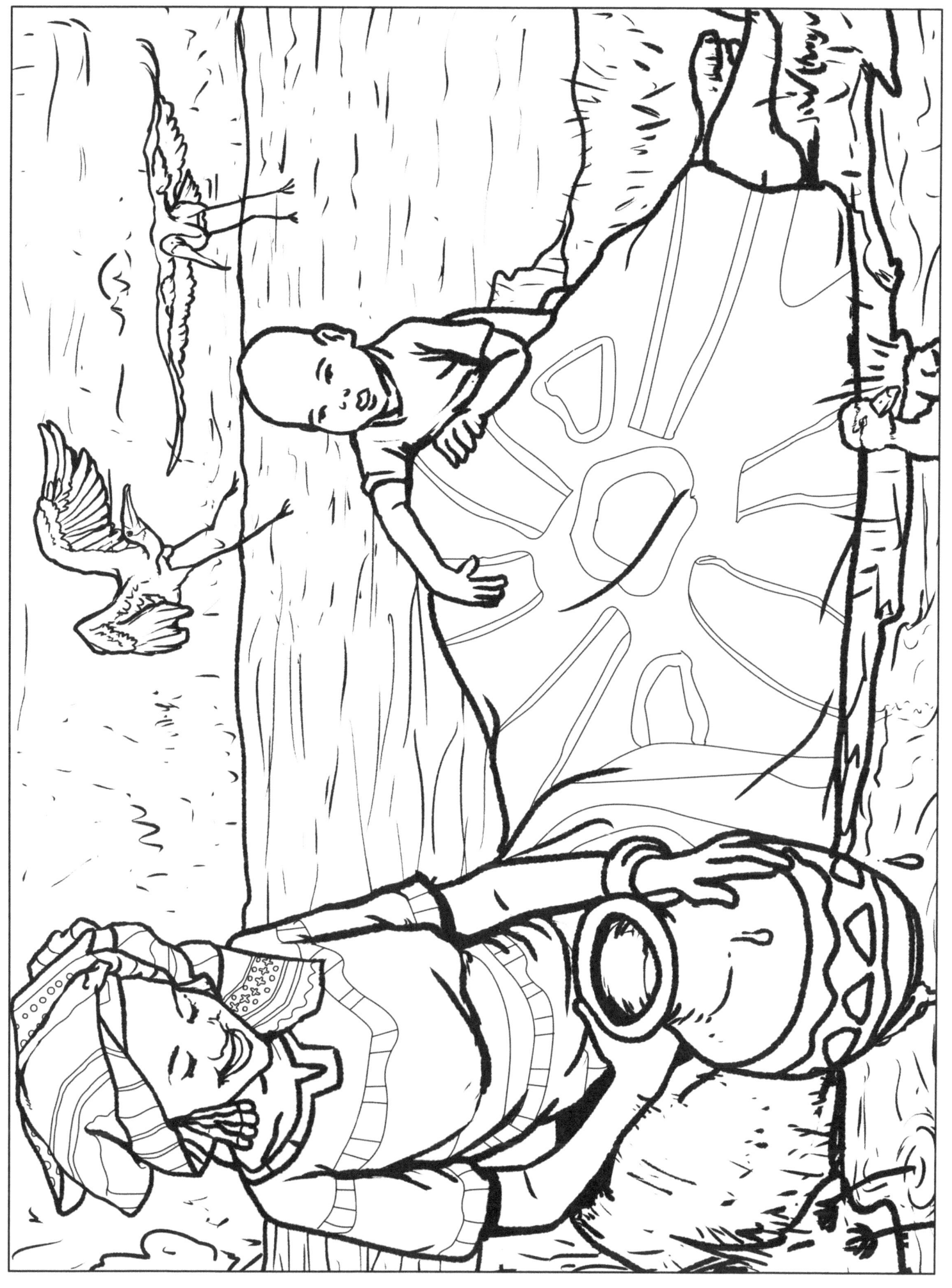

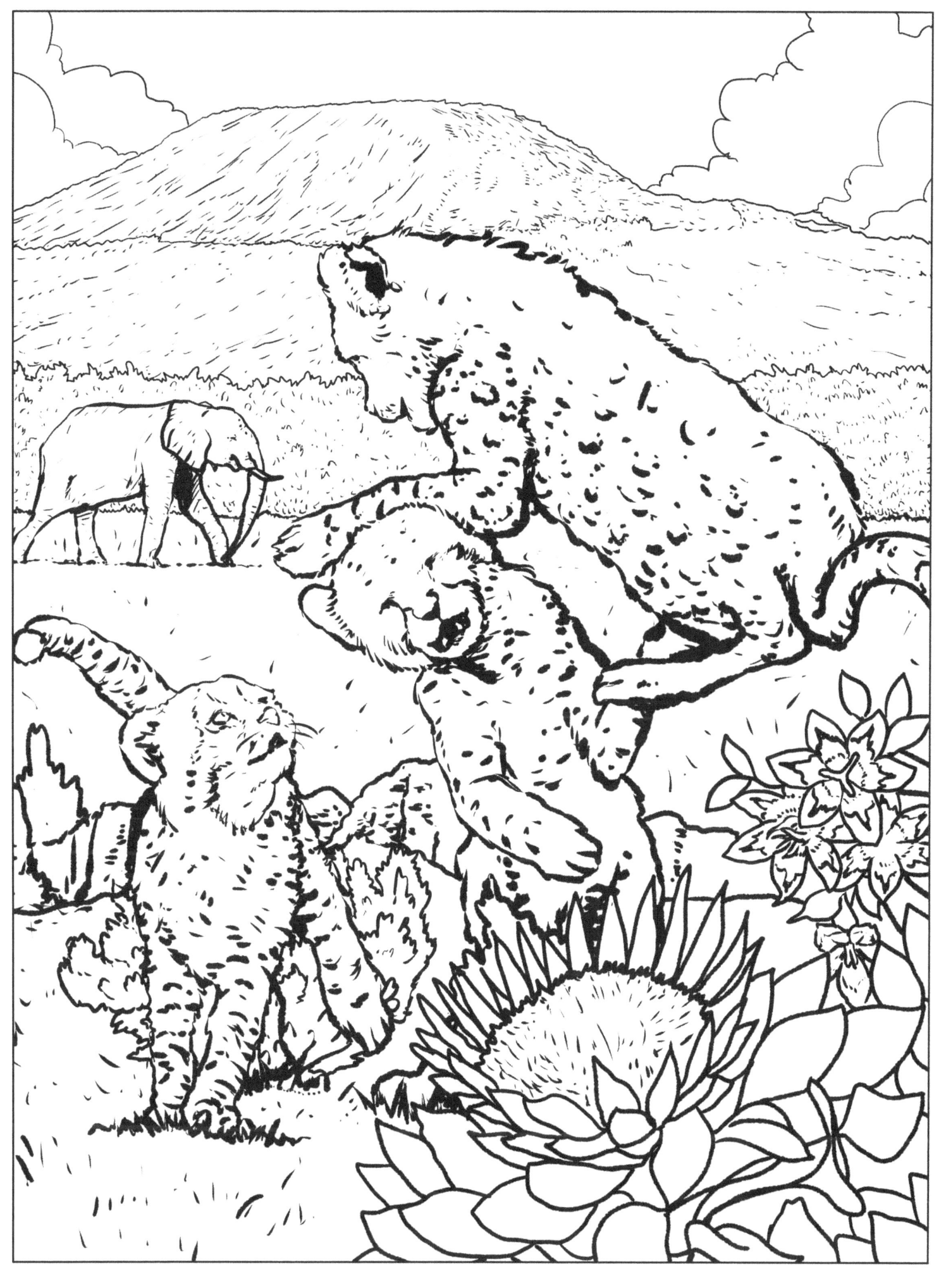

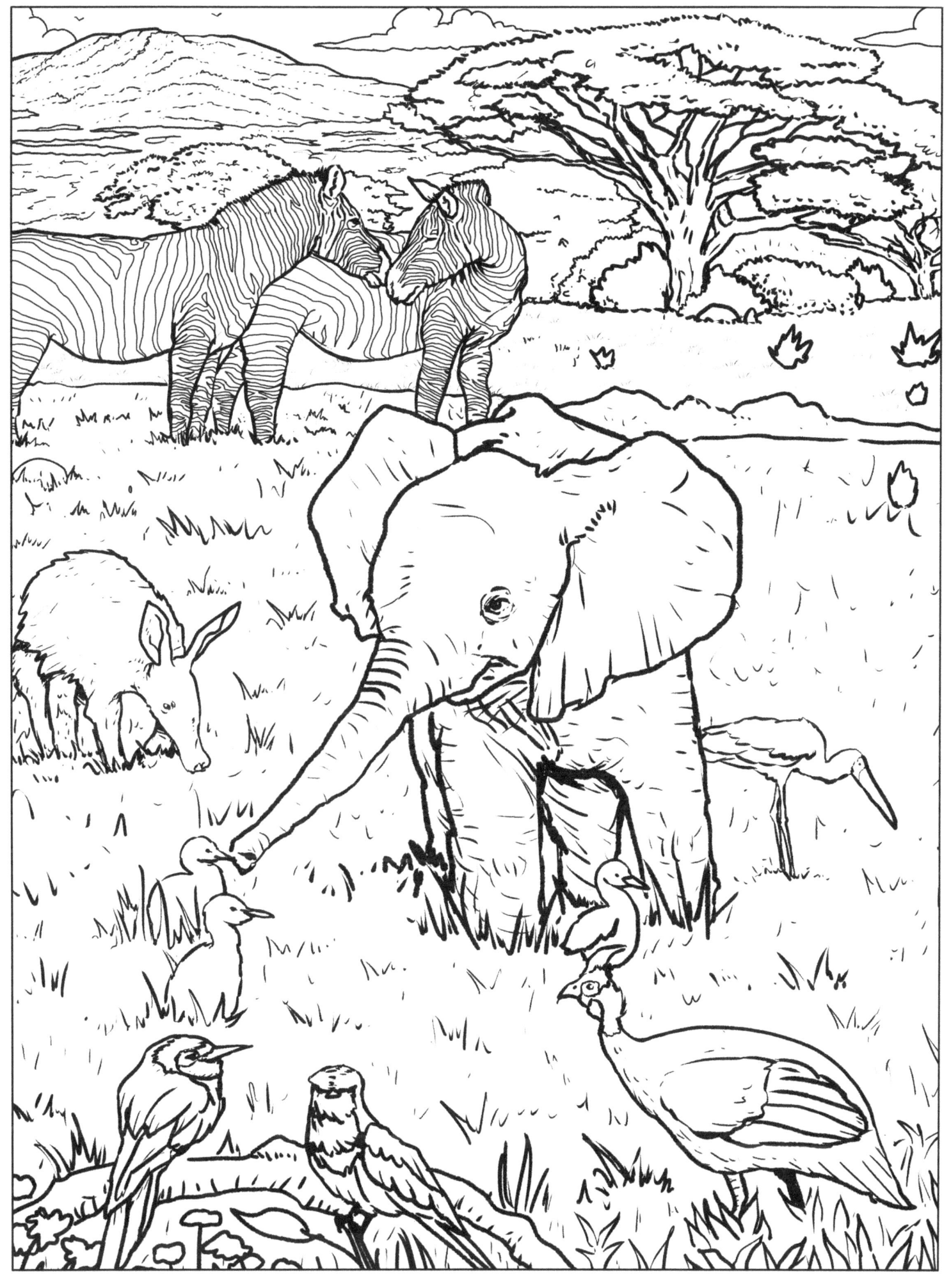

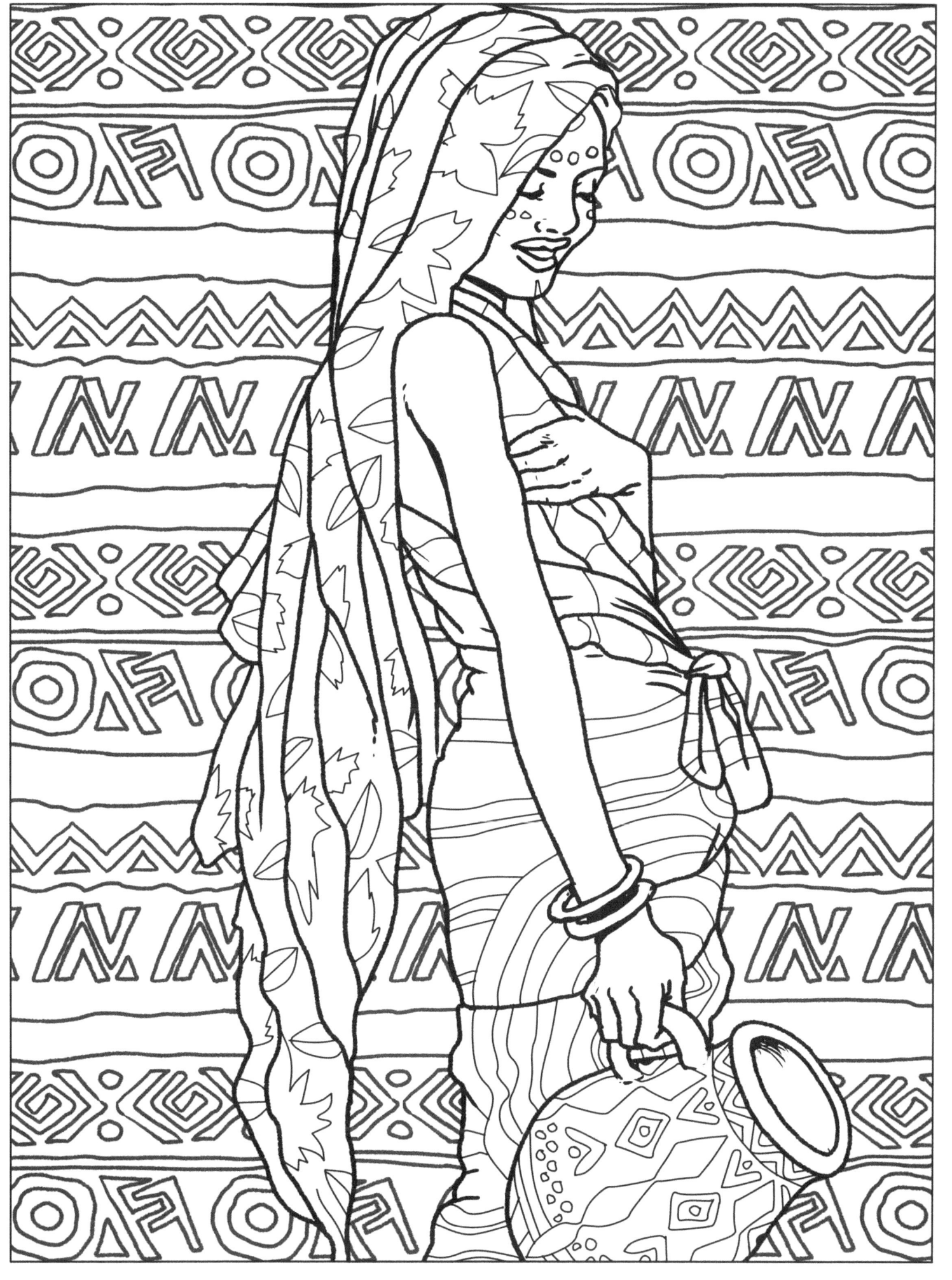

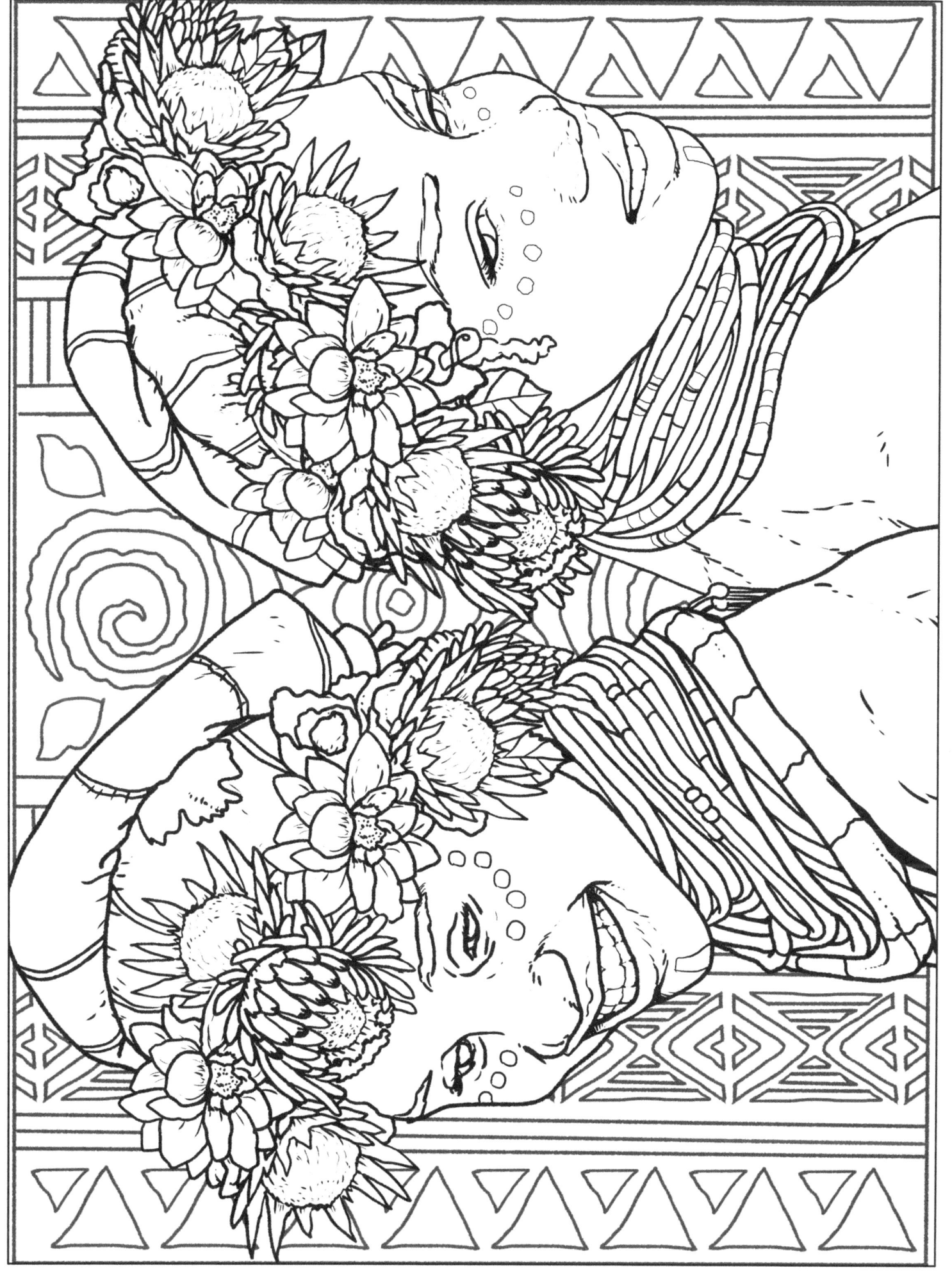

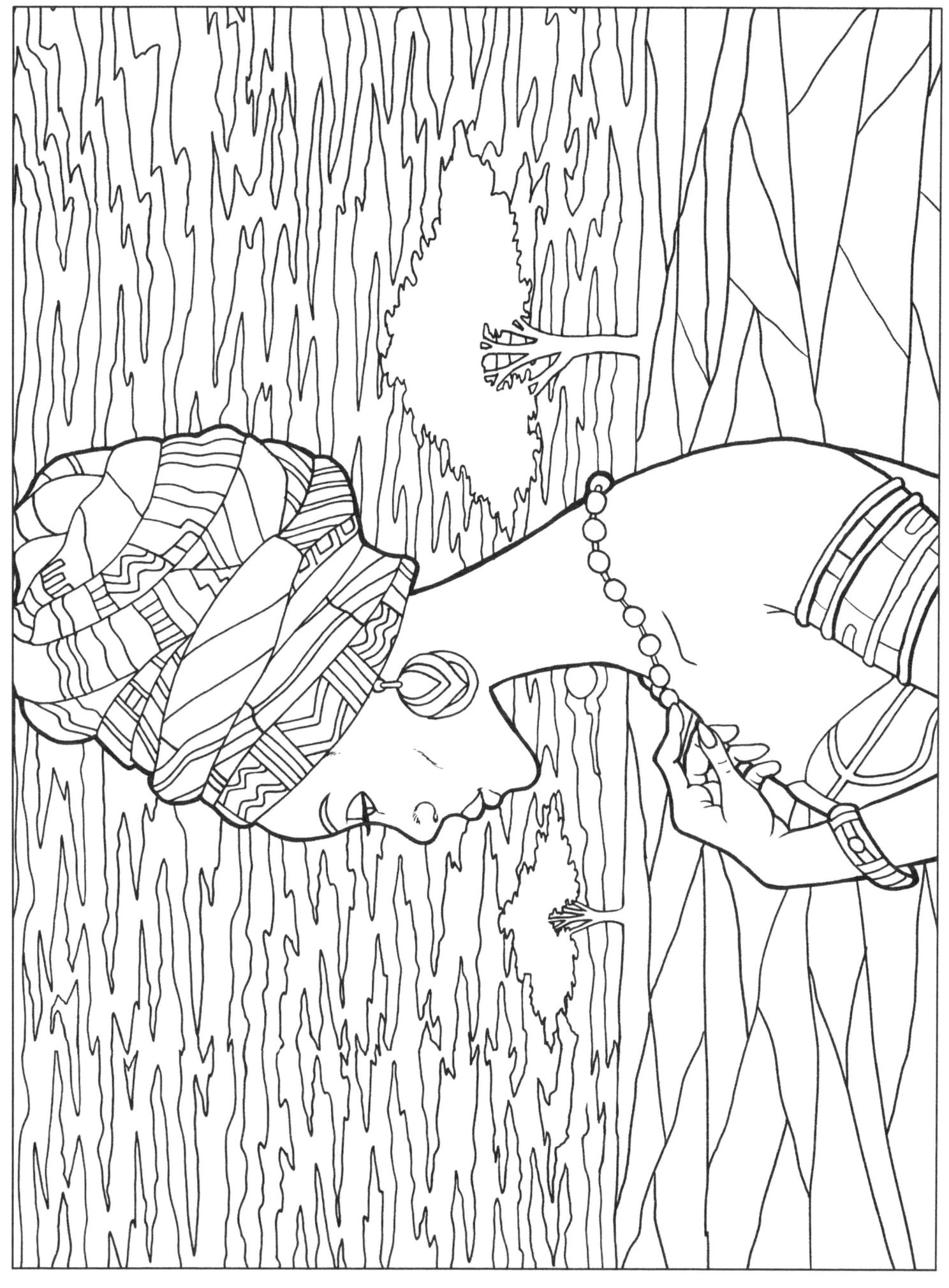

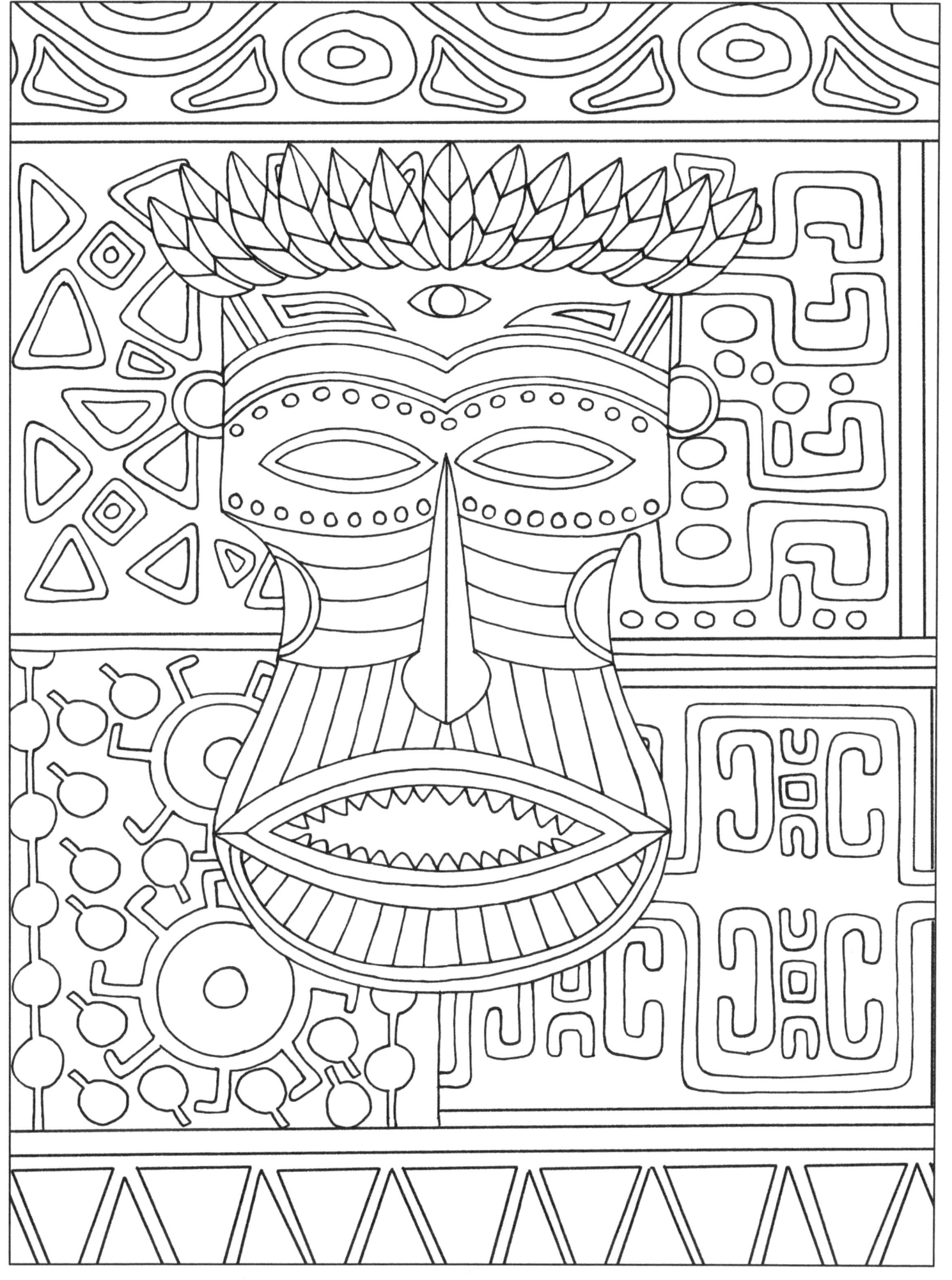

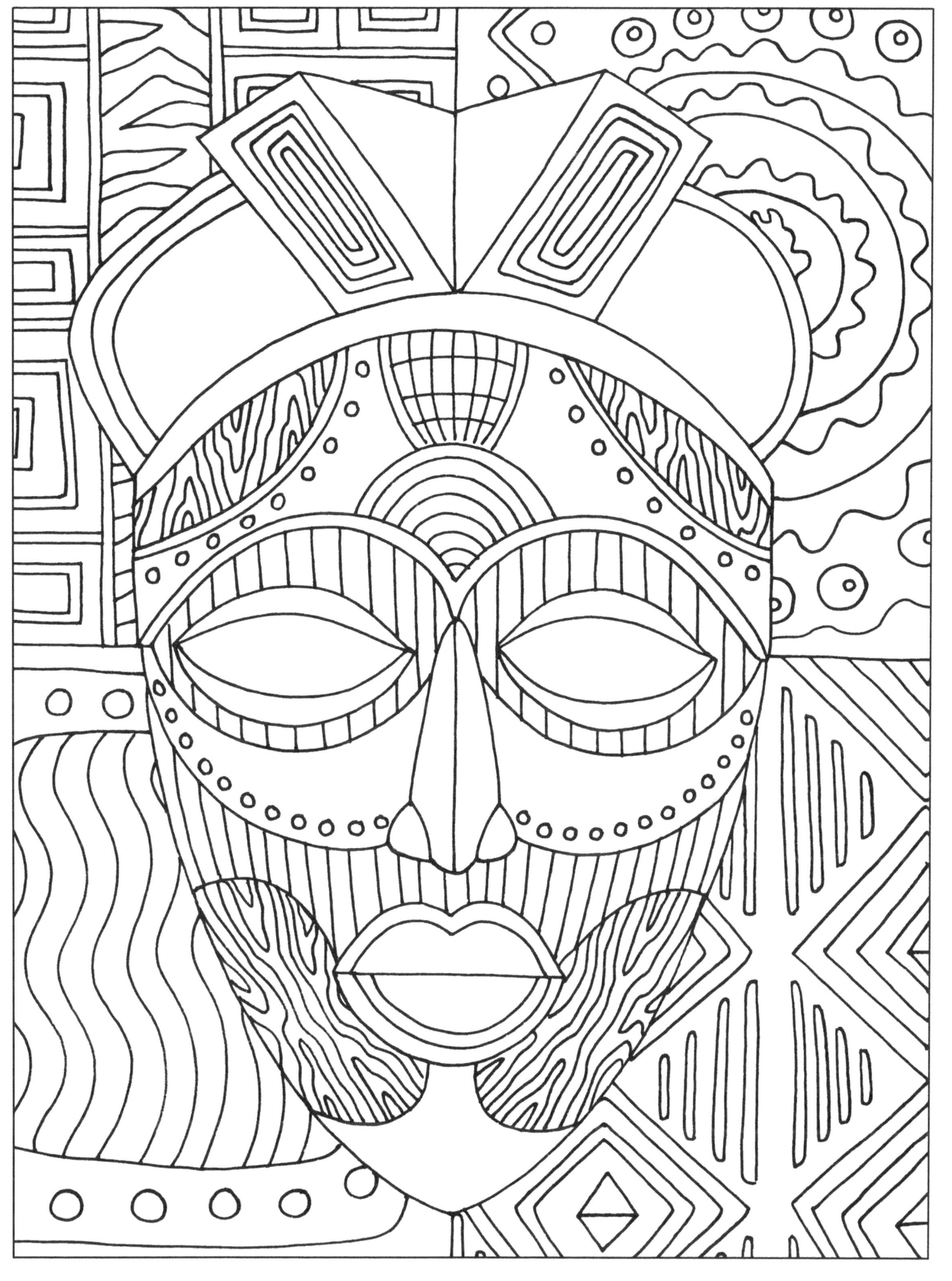

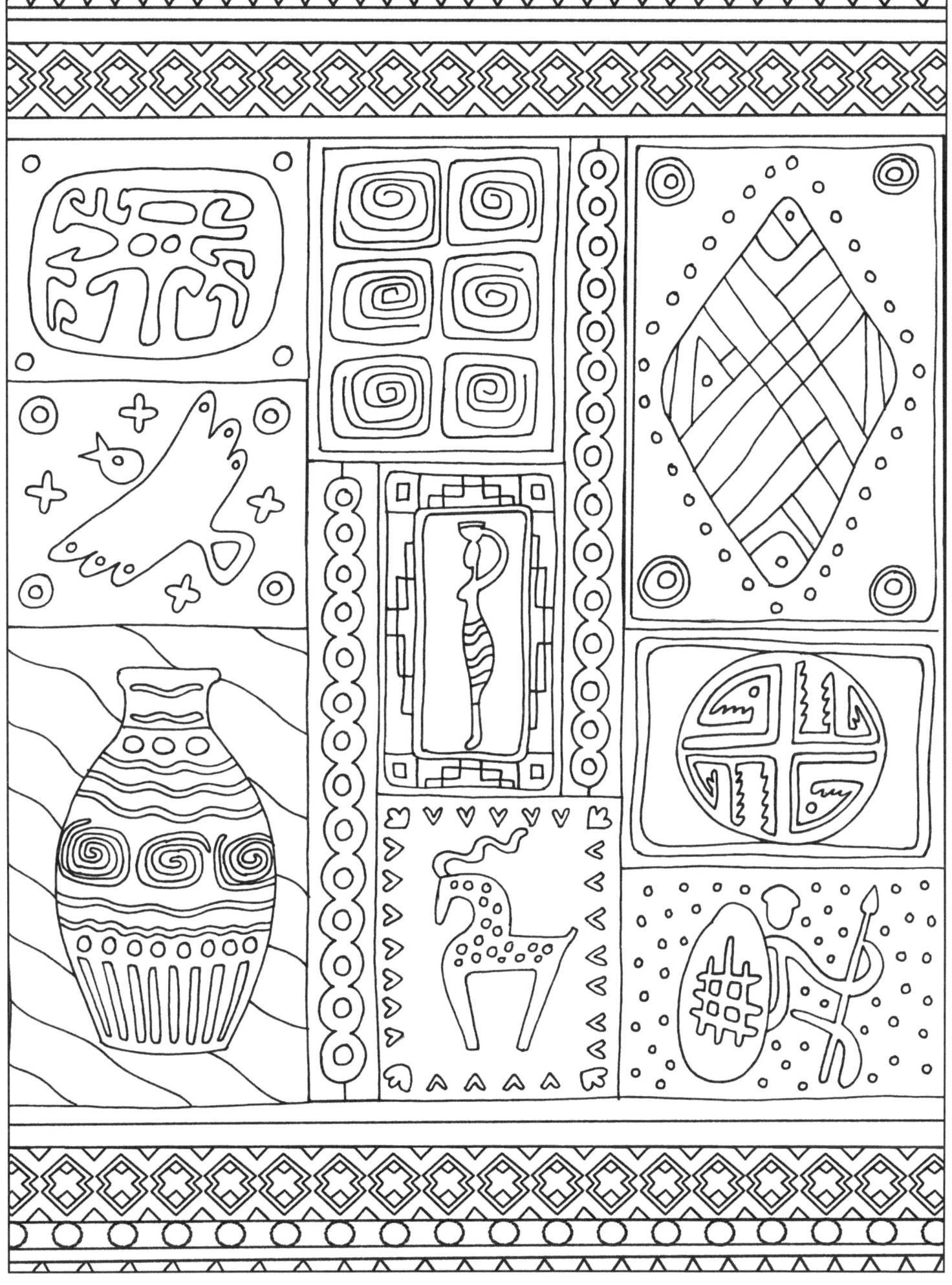

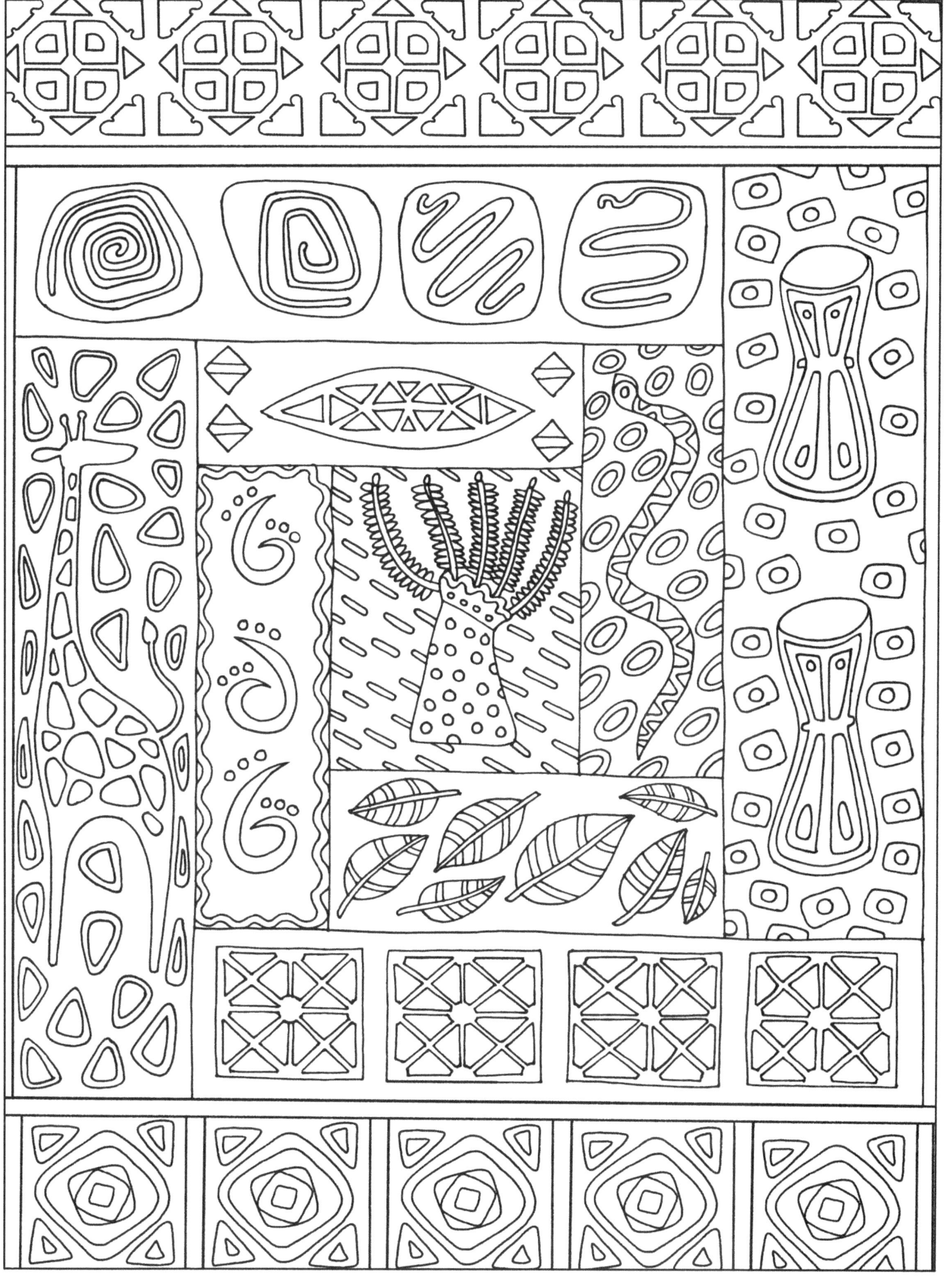

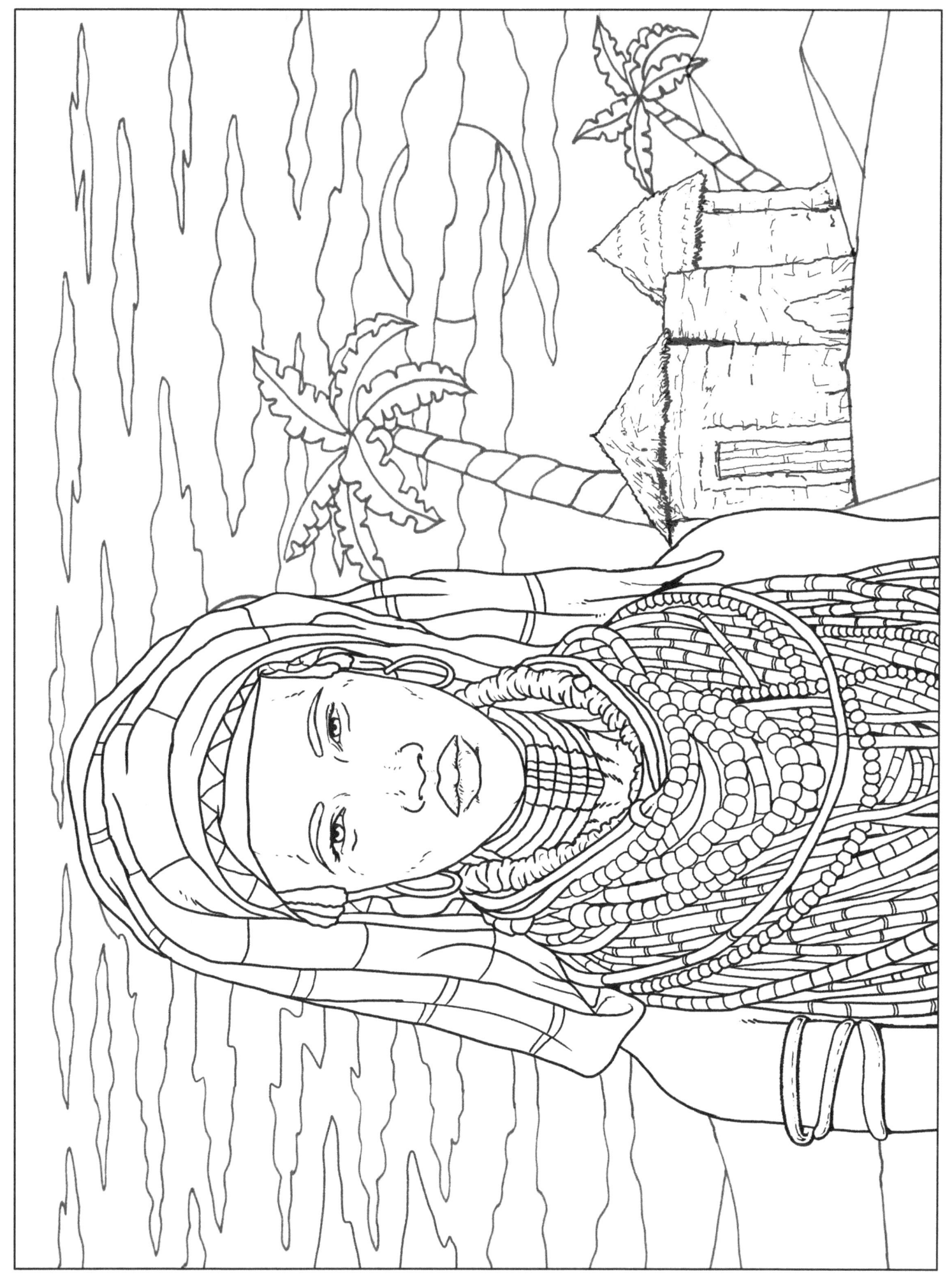

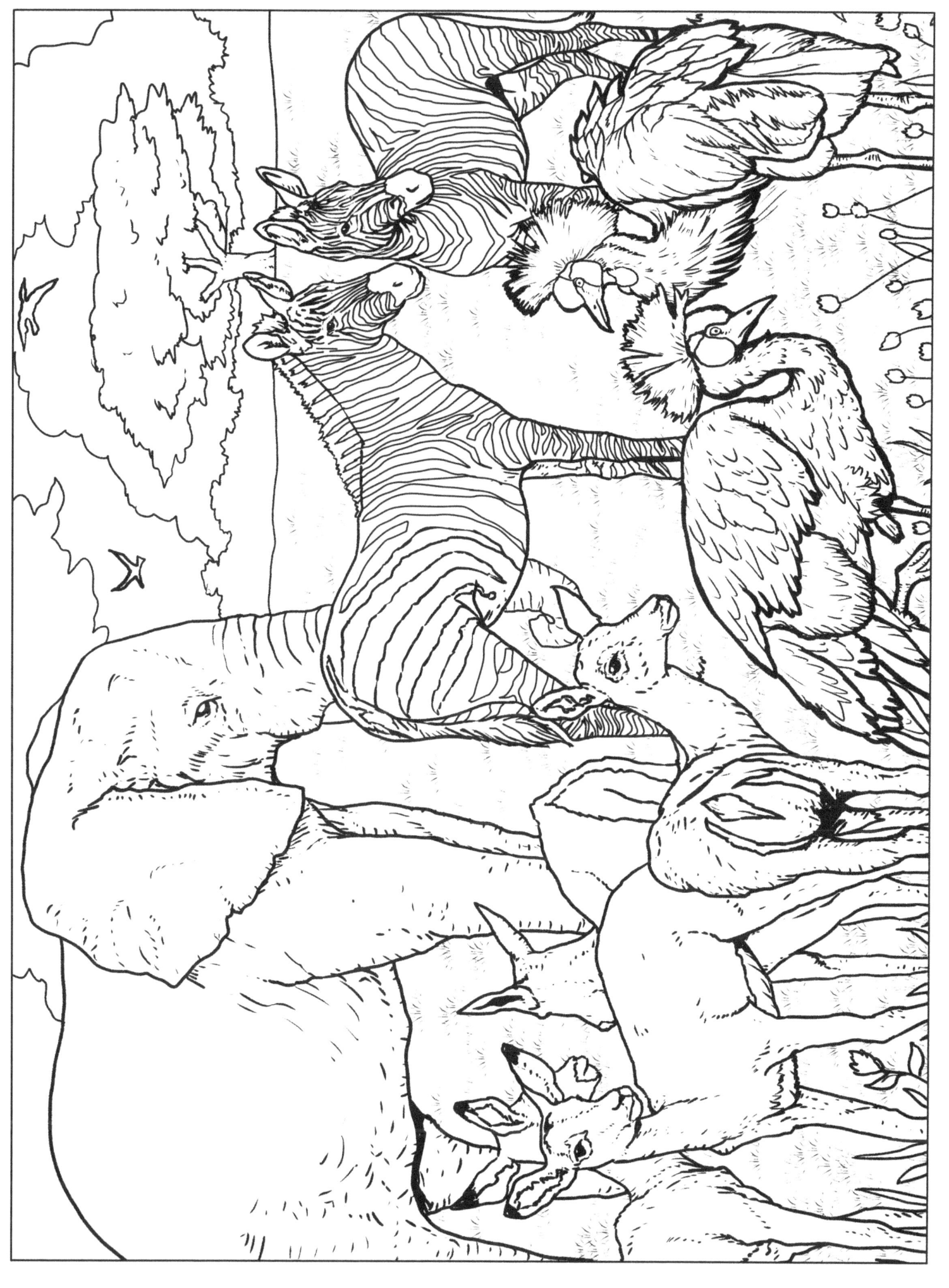

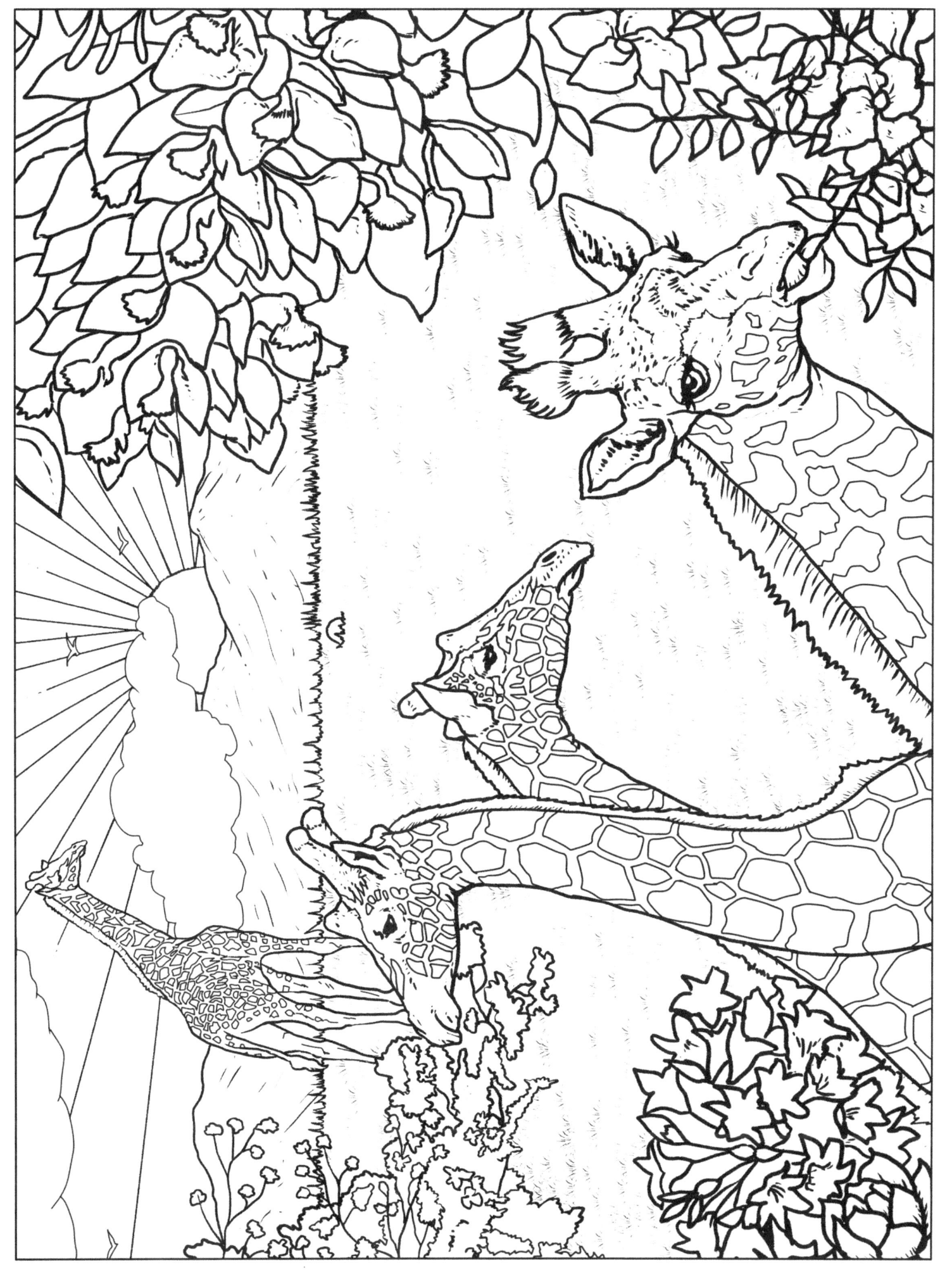

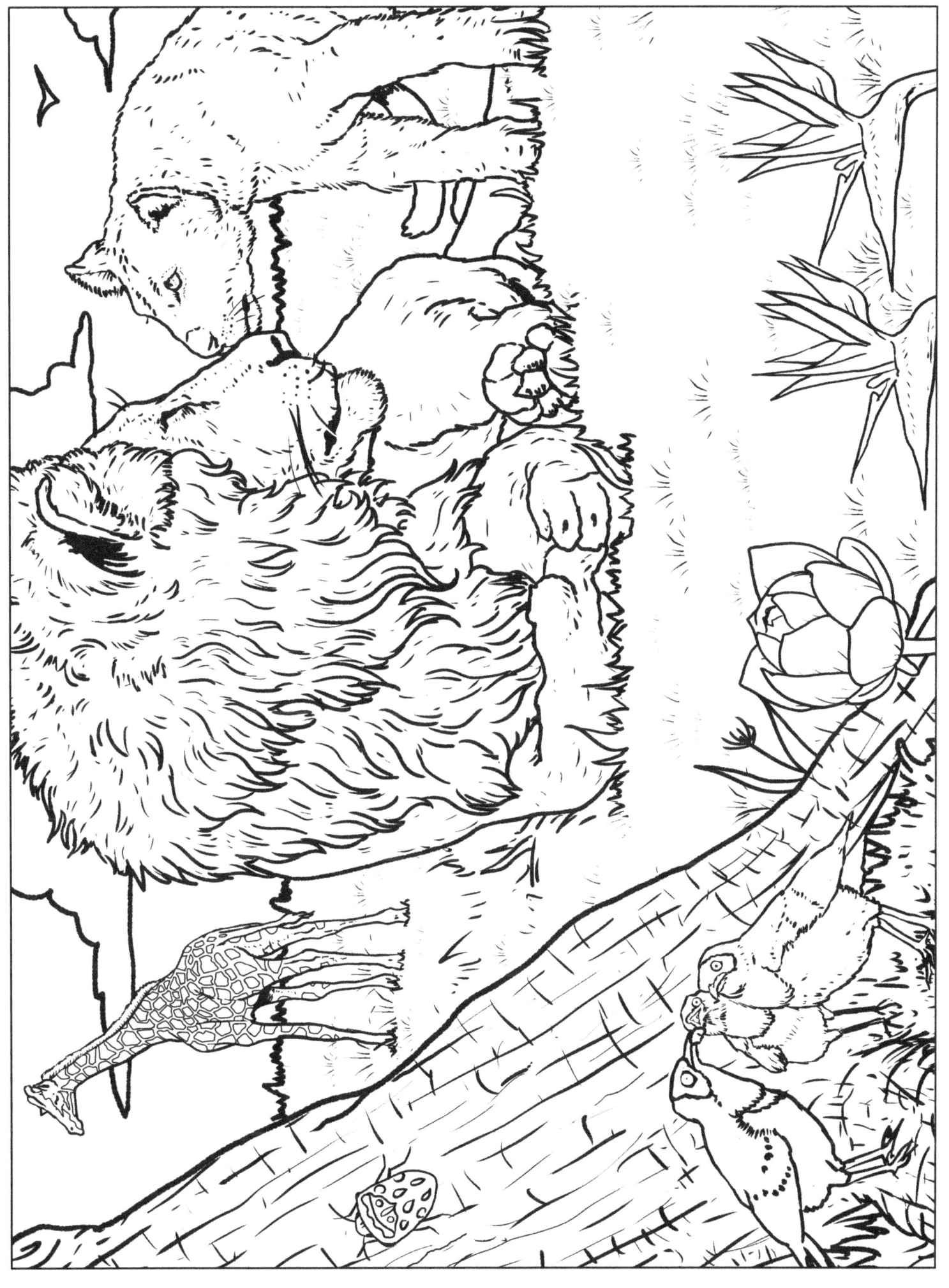

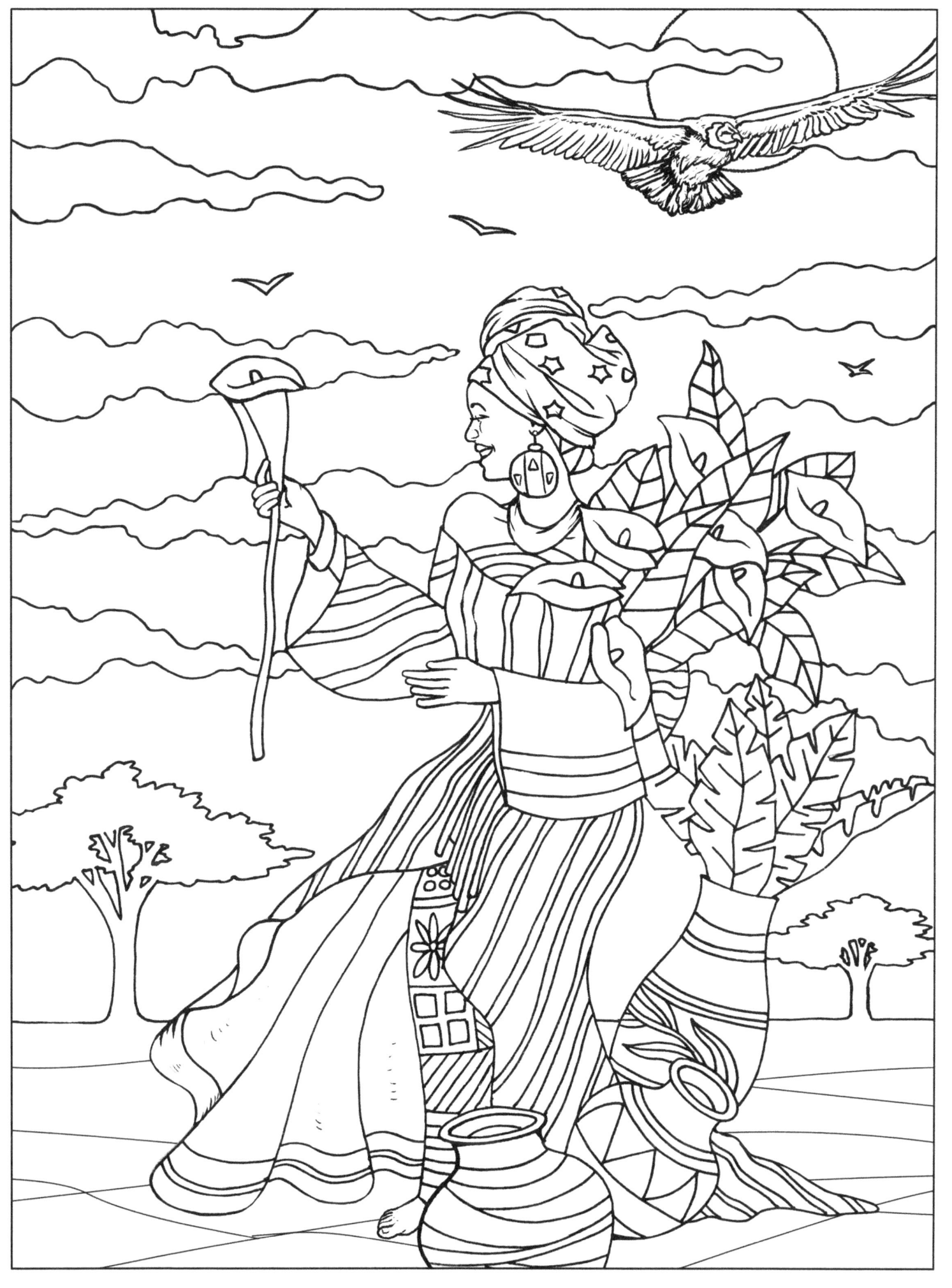

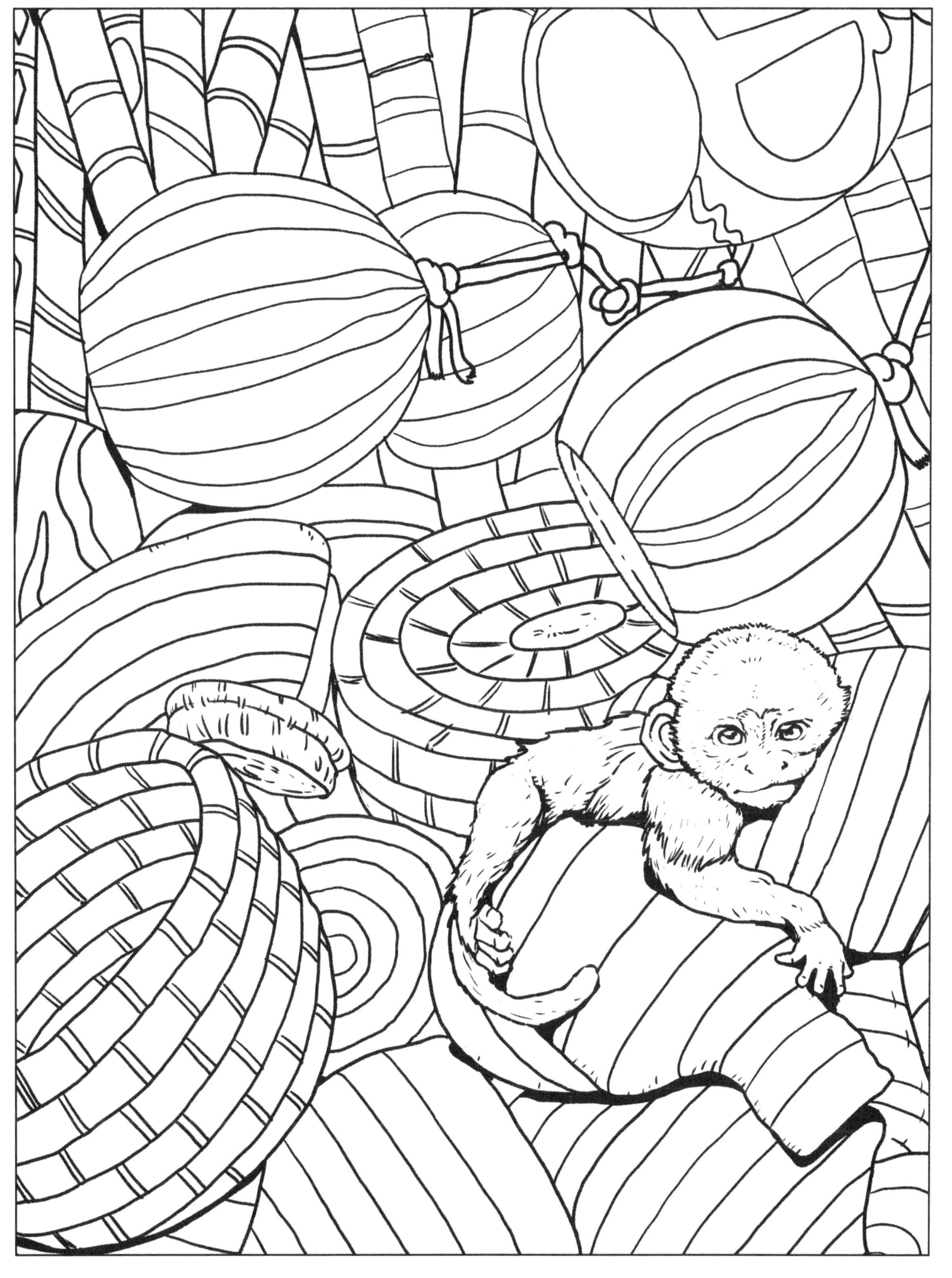

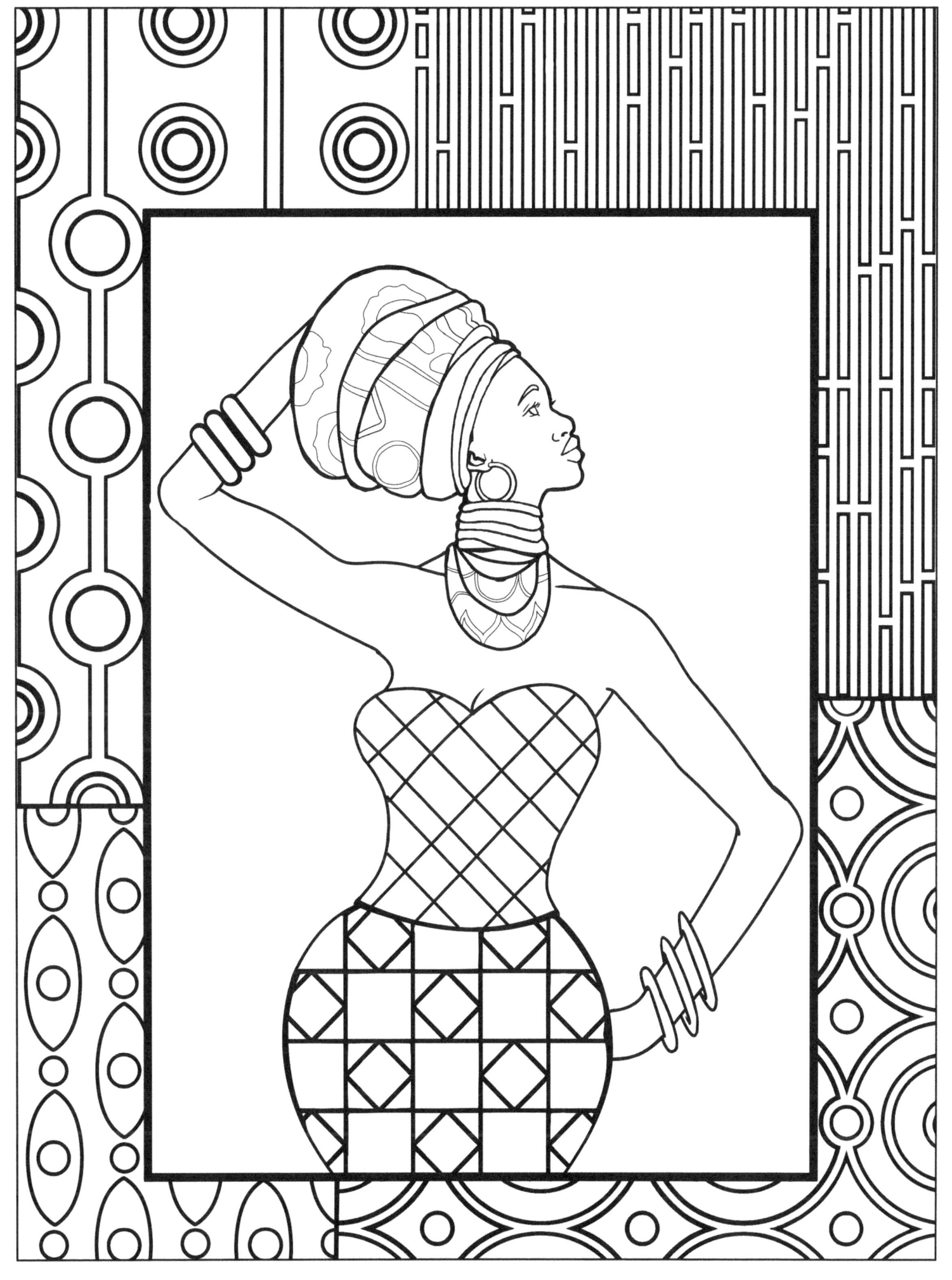

Thank you for supporting
ZenMaster Coloring Books

Your support means the world to us,
and we're thrilled to have you embark on this
creative journey with us.

Our small company strives to make a
BIG difference by helping those
who may be less fortunate.

This is why we proudly hire struggling
artists from around the world!

Our goal is to provide financial support to artists and
their families by enabling them to pursue their passions
and share their hard work and limitless talent with you!

Help support our hard working artists
by leaving a positive review on Amazon!

And follow us on Facebook for updates and
FREE COLORING PAGES!
https://www.facebook.com/zenmastercoloringbooks/

Check out more of our books at:
amazon.com/author/zenmastercoloringbooks

Free Bonus Page!
from:

Japanese
Art and Designs
Coloring Book for Adults

https://www.amazon.com/dp/153726771x

Also available in color by numbers!!

https://www.amazon.com/dp/1981642242

And 5x8" Travel Size

https://www.amazon.com/dp/1539444066

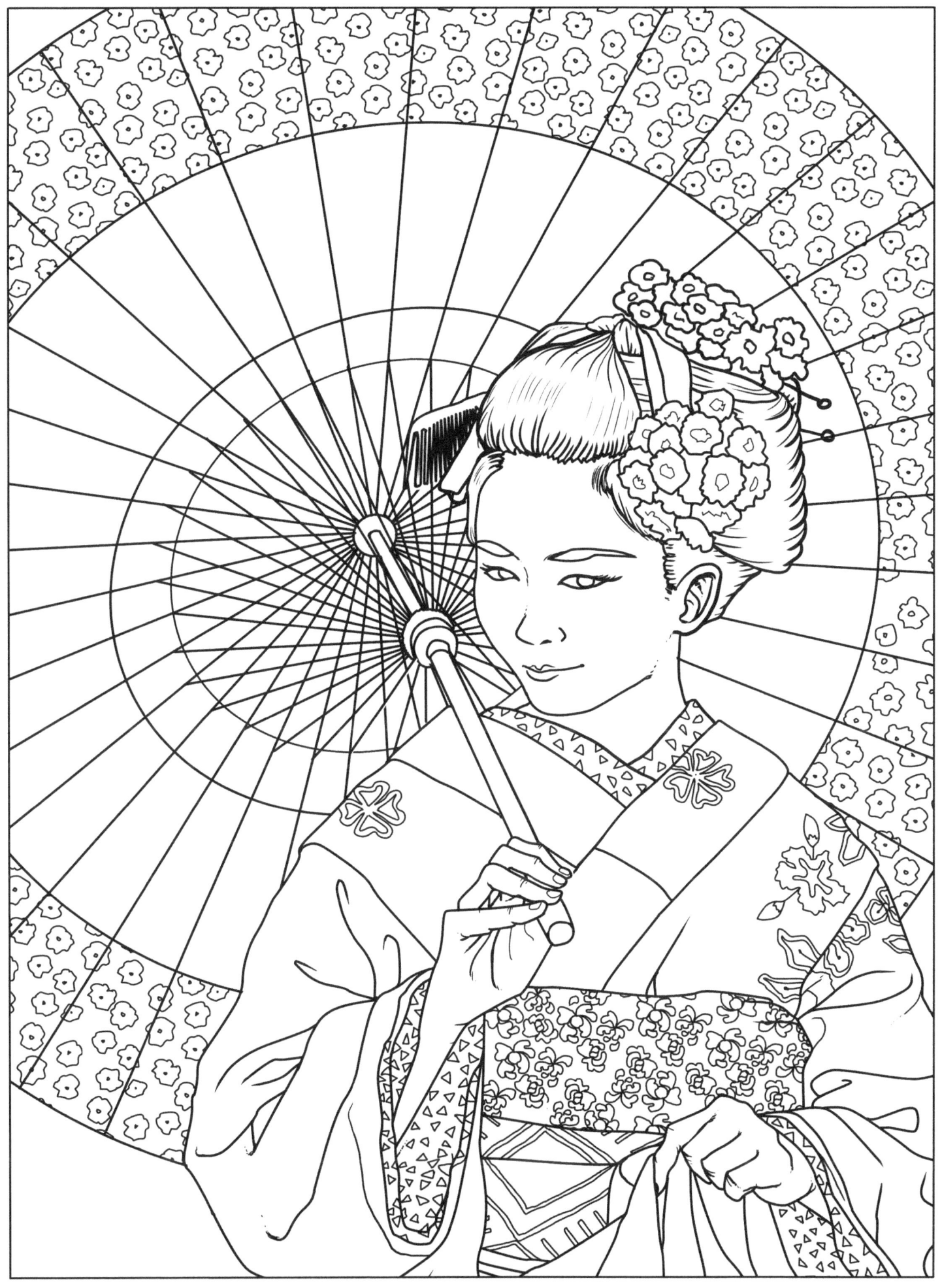

Free Bonus Page!
from:

India Art & Designs

Adult Coloring Book

https://www.amazon.com/dp/1537731114

Also available in color by numbers!!

https://www.amazon.com/dp/173130420X

And 5x8" Travel Size

https://www.amazon.com/dp/1539444295

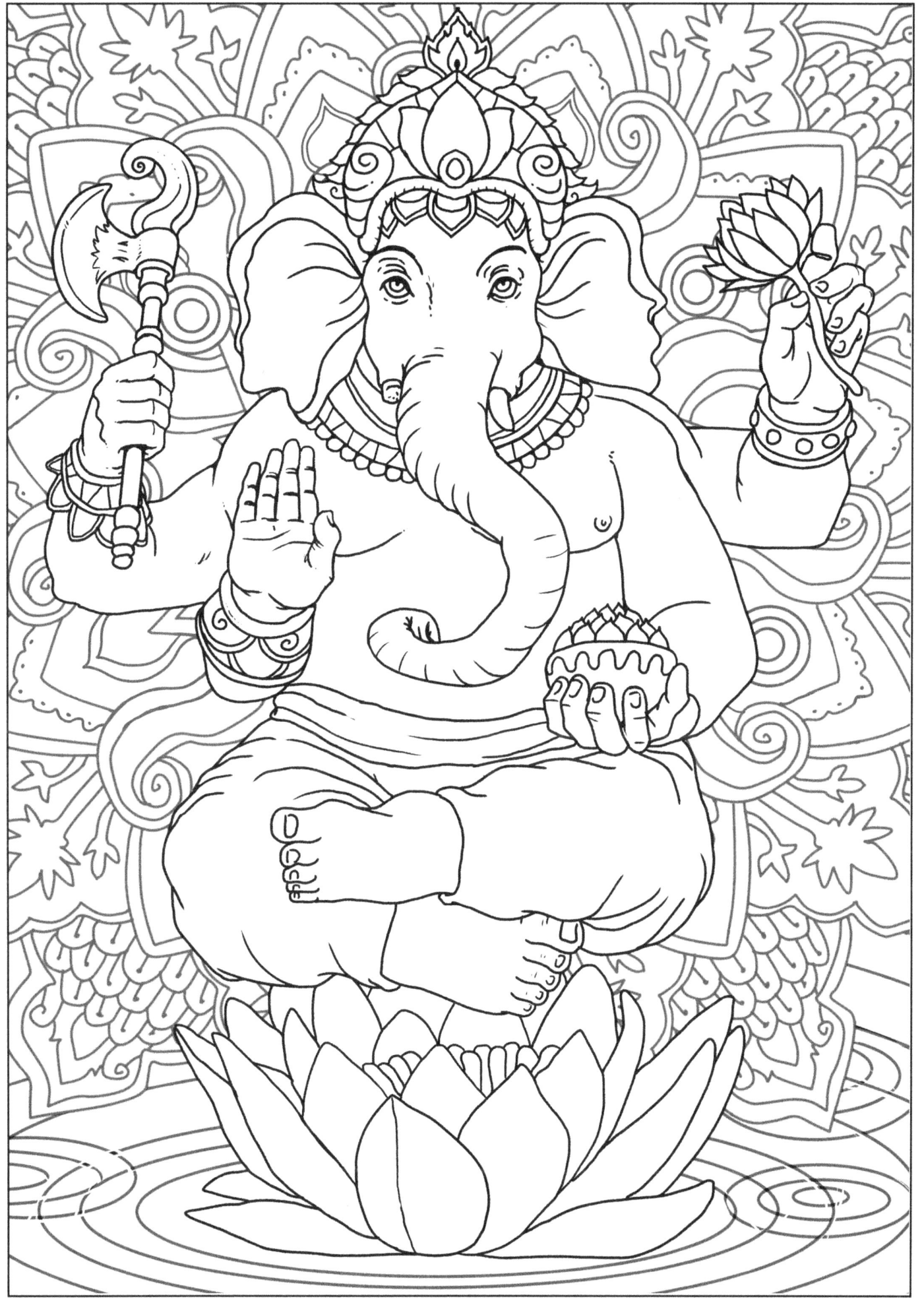

Free Bonus Page!
from:

Native American
Coloring Book for Adults

https://www.amazon.com/dp/1545034478

Also available in color by numbers!!
https://amzn.com/dp/1977866379

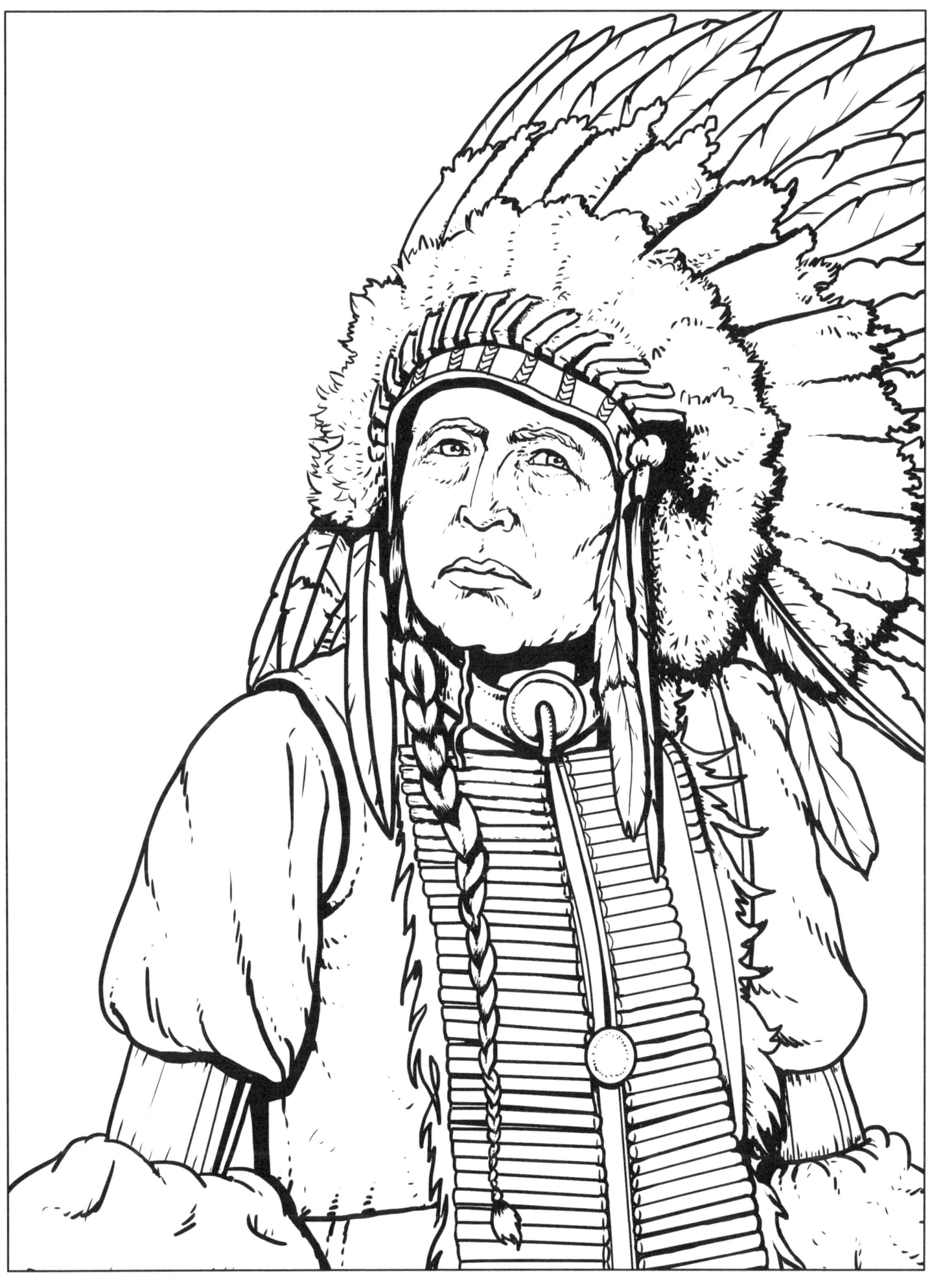

Free Bonus Page!
from:

National Parks
Coloring Book for Adults

https://www.amazon.com/dp/1690162821

Also available in color by numbers!!

https://www.amazon.com/dp/1690168536

And 5x8" Travel Size

https://www.amazon.com/dp/1690176016

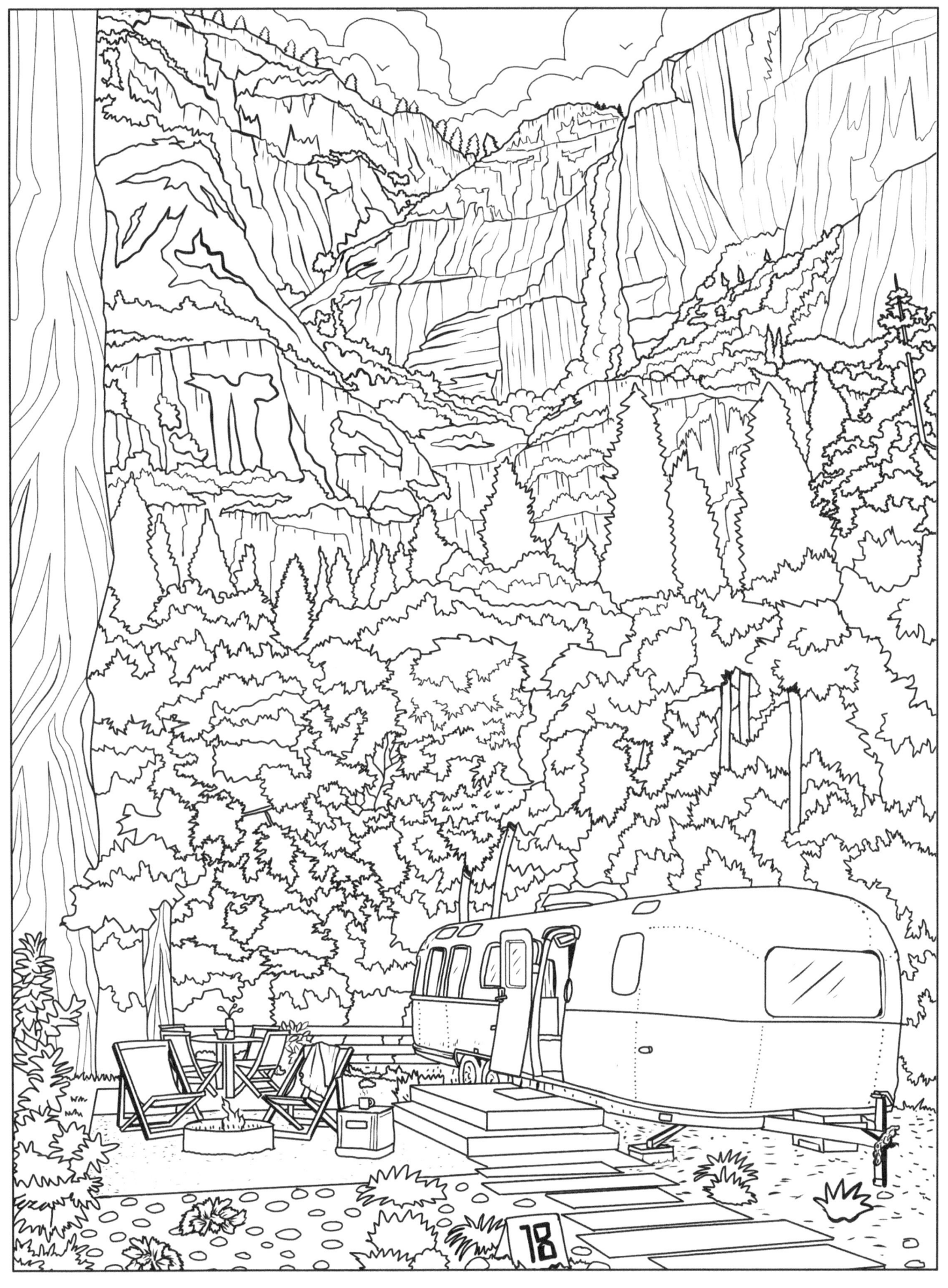

Free Bonus Page!
from:

Extreme dot to dot book of

Butterflies and Flowers

https://amzn.com/dp/1717596746

Also available in color by numbers!!

https://www.amazon.com/dp/1977932398

And a non-numbered edition

https://www.amazon.com/dp/1977882978

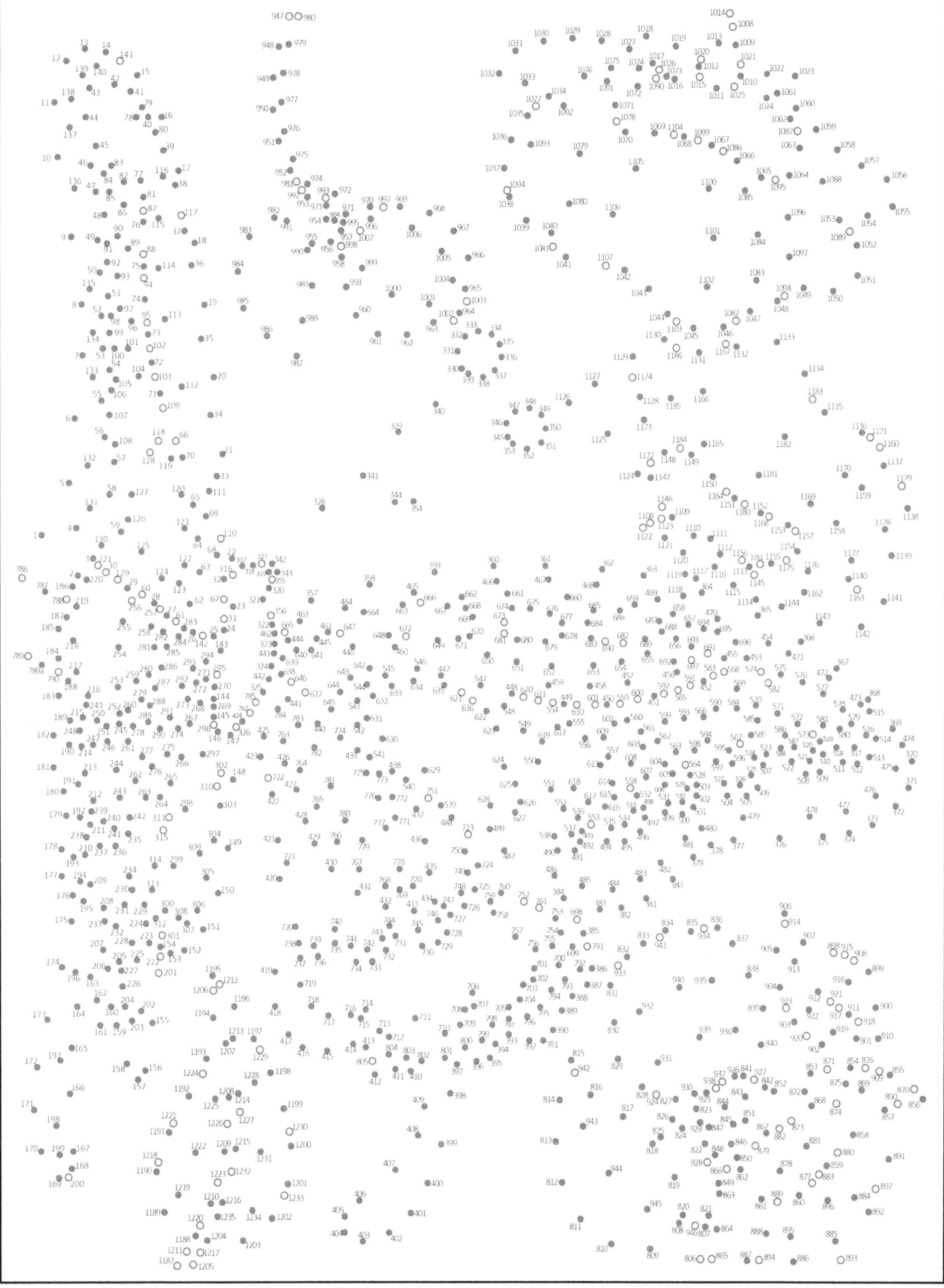

Free Bonus Page!
from:

Zen Coloring Notebook

https://www.amazon.com/dp/1535457015

Available in 9 different colors!

Also available in 5x8" journal size

https://www.amazon.com/dp/1535540591